Series editor
ALISTAIR
BRYCE-CLEGG

fantastic ideas for
storytelling

JUDIT HORVATH

Featherstone
An imprint of Bloomsbury Publishing Plc

50 Bedford Square
London
WC1B 3DP
UK

1385 Broadway
New York
NY 10018
USA

www.bloomsbury.com

FEATHERSTONE and the Feather logo are trademarks of Bloomsbury Publishing Plc

First published in Great Britain 2017

Copyright © Judit Horvath, 2017
Photos copyright © Judit Horvath, 2017 / © Shutterstock 2017

Judit Horvath has asserted her right under the Copyright, Designs and Patents Act, 1988,
to be identified as Author of this work.

A catalogue record for this book is available from the British Library.

ISBN
PB: 978-1-4729-4160-2
ePDF: 978-1-4729-4161-9

2 4 6 8 10 9 7 5 3 1

Printed and bound in India by Replika Press Pvt. Ltd.

This book is produced using paper that is made from wood grown in managed, sustainable forests.
It is natural, renewable and recyclable. The logging and manufacturing processes conform to the
environmental regulations of the country of origin.

To find out more about our authors and books visit www.bloomsbury.com. Here you will find extracts,
author interviews, details of forthcoming events and the option to sign up for our newsletters.

Contents

Introduction

The main aim of the book

Amongst many popular activities in early years, listening to and telling stories remains one of the most popular things to do. Apart from being fun and exciting, storytelling has many functions for a child's growing mind and plays an important part in language and communication. Storytelling is one of the most powerful ways for developing human thinking and to help children make sense of the world around them. Children often retell their adventures as stories, from a simple account of having dinner to major life events. Stories organise moments from the past and as they happen, and both the story and its telling convey important information about the self, relationships, and thoughts and feelings in the children's personal life.

The main aim of this book is to introduce simple but creative ideas to prompt and aid storytelling for and with the children. A growing number of research studies have shown that, in some cultures at least, parents and their babies talk about the past and future much more frequently and in greater depth than we had ever expected (Nelson 1989, Engel 1995). Studies have also shown that social interaction is not only the site of emerging abilities such as conversation and storytelling, but that the input of conversational partners can have a strong influence on what a child learns (Snow and Ferguson 1977, Miller and Sperry 1988).

Learning through storytelling

Storytelling has many benefits, and not just for the children: telling and listening to stories in a variety of ways will strengthen the relationship between storytellers and listeners. It instills virtues in the children: by telling children stories that come with a meaningful message, qualities like integrity, courage, honesty and so on will be inculcated from an early age.

Stories will make children aware of their own culture and roots. Recounting stories from their own childhood and about various activities and celebrations from their own lives will make children more aware of the different customs and traditions prevalent in their families. Sharing stories about various family members will help them learn about their lineage. At the same time, stories also broaden the children's world, exposing them to different cultures and countries.

Storytelling enhances verbal proficiency, helps acquaint children with language as well as helping them to learn new words and phrases, whilst also improving listening skills and strengthening attention span.

Storytelling encourages creativity and imagination, so children become open to ideas and free thinking. Storytelling sharpens memory and increases concentration. Storytelling, as a regular activity, can help children to enjoy and better understand what they are reading. It also encourages children to be confident when asking questions, learning the art of following their own curiosity. Ultimately, storytelling teaches children a really important life-skill: it helps them to face difficult situations and aids the process of getting to know and control their own feelings.

The structure of the book

The pages are all organised in the same way. Before you start any activity, read through everything on the page so you are familiar with the whole activity and what you might need to plan in advance.

What you need lists the resources required for the activity. These are likely to be readily available in most settings or can be bought/made easily.

What to do tells you step-by-step what you need to do to compete the activity.

Observation questions prompt the practitioner to evaluate how the children are engaging with one another and the activity itself, with links to the EYFS Statutory Framework.

The **Health & Safety** tips are often obvious, but safety can't be overstressed. In many cases there are no specific hazards involved in completing the activity, and your usual health and safety measures should be enough. In others there are particular issues to be noted and addressed.

Taking it forward gives ideas for additional activities on the same theme, or for developing the activity further. These will be particularly useful for things that have gone especially well or where children show a real interest. In many cases they use the same resources, and in every case they have been designed to extend learning and broaden the children's experiences.

Finally, **What's in it for the children?** tells you (and others) briefly how the suggested activities contribute to learning.

Clay story toys

What you need:

- Clay
- Pebbles to create the body
- Decorations to create characteristics such as: fabric pieces, beads, yarn, buttons, matchsticks

What to do:

1. Choose a story to read and discuss the story characters during circle time, including any specific characteristics that make them similar or different.

2. Give each child a piece of clay and a pebble or assign a particular character to a small group of children.

3. Roll the clay into a ball (smaller than the pebble), and secure it on the top of the pebble to create a body.

4. Use additional items to create specific characters. Make hair, eyes, arms, legs.

5. Compare the characters and make notes about similarities and differences of children themselves.

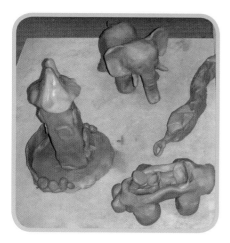

What's in it for the children?

Children will enjoy each other's company whilst learning about taking turns, co-operation and working in a team.

Taking it forward

- Children can present their own show and act out events.
- Children can make the characters of a story such as *The Gruffalo* and then compare how they see/make things similarly or differently.
- Make characters of the children themselves, using photos and mirror.

Observation questions

- Can the child follow simple instructions?
- Is the child engaging in stories?

paper bag puppets

What you need:

- Paper bag
- Coloured paper
- Paint, crayons, pencils
- Goggly eyes or buttons
- Yarn
- Glue

What to do:

1. Chose a side of the paper bag that provides a flat, good-sized surface for the children to draw, paint or stick a face on. When using a paper bag with flaps (bags that are longer on one side, having an added, folding material on the top as closure) the flap can either be taped to secure from opening, or built within the character used as ears, tongue etc.

2. Use art supplies such as paint, crayons, or pencils invite the children to draw facial features on the flap.

3. For eyes, glue on two googly eyes or buttons (or you can draw them on the bag). You can also draw or glue fabric scraps or coloured paper on.

4. Draw or stick on a nose, mouth, and maybe a tongue!

5. Add hair by cutting some lengths of yarn. Glue them on to the top edge or the front of the flap, near the top.

6. To use the puppet, put a hand into the bag and wiggle your fingers/move your hand up and down to make the puppet 'talk.'

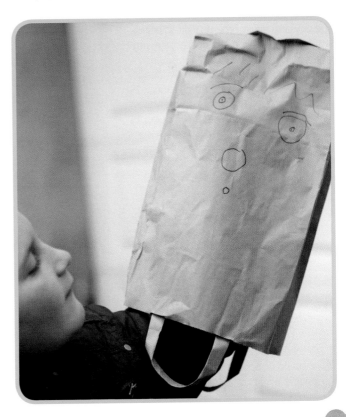

What's in it for the children?

Children can develop listening and understanding skills by paying attention to small details in stories. This will also develop their ability to describe things when they communicate, as their vocabulary expands.

Taking it forward

- Children can create their own movie by filming their puppet show.
- Children can make their own paper bag from recycled paper.

Observation questions

- How does the child engage with the activity?

Small world storytelling

What you need:

- Builder's tray or very large shallow container
- Soil, sand, pebbles
- Moss, leaves
- Sticks
- Corks
- Pine cones, conkers
- Small world characters

What to do:

1. Discuss the story or the story scene that will be set e.g. *Little Red Riding Hood's* forest, and ask the children to sketch out their ideas.

2. Place the builder's tray or container safely on a table or on the ground outside.

3. Scatter soil around in the bottom of the tray, then add the ground features making partitions with fingers; such as Red Riding Hood's house, grandma's house.

4. Work alongside the children as they play and encourage them to act out the story.

5. Add play characters, or make them from any material available in the setting.

6. Encourage children to think imaginatively and to find items to represent characters and other objects, for example a twig from the outdoor area to use as a tree.

What's in it for the children?

Children can select equipment to build and develop environments, retell familiar stories talking about key characters, and sequence events. They can work alone or co-operatively, talk about their ideas and negotiate roles with others, and use language to link ideas and recreate experiences. They can explore concepts of space and size, make maps and plans, become deeply involved in play and develop ideas and understanding over a period of time.

Taking it forward

- Divide the class into small groups or pairs. Ask them to set the scene for the same story and compare their viewpoints such as what each think is important from the story etc.

Observation questions

- Can the children work as a part of a group?

- Do children have an understanding of basic concepts such as, how people live, how people are different from animals, how animals live?

Spoon puppet theatre

What you need:

- Wooden or plastic spoon
- Felt tip pen
- Glue
- Masking tape
- Pipe cleaners
- String
- Yarn
- Coloured tissue paper
- Fabric pieces

What to do:

1. Chose a story and list the characters (animals, people, fairytale/mystical characters and so on).

2. Make the puppet's face by drawing on the inside of the spoon using felt tip pens. Draw whatever expression suits the puppet you're making: happy, sad, angry, poking a tongue out etc.

3. Decorate the puppet. Use masking tape to stick pieces of tissue paper and scrap material to make the clothing (or scales, armour etc.). Tape is a lot less messy than glue and features can be easily changed.

4. Stick the craft items to the handle of the spoon to create a costume for the puppet.

5. Add pipe cleaners for arms and legs by twisting them around the handle.

6. Add other features, such as hair, beard etc.

7. Make more puppets and put on a puppet show!

What's in it for the children?

Children will have an opportunity to develop empathy. They will have to listen and take turns, respecting the opinion of others when creating a production as a joint effort.

Taking it forward

- Create characters based on the children and act out problematic situations (real or hypothetical) within the class to communicate rules and expectations.

Observation questions

- Can the children recognise and represent non-verbal expressions linked to feelings?

- Can the children pretend and engage in imaginative play?

Sock puppet

What you need:

- Socks
- Googly eyes, buttons
- Scissors
- Hot melt glue and glue gun
- Additional fabric, felt
- String
- Yarn
- Pipe cleaners

What to do:

1. Discuss your chosen story and ask the children to draw sketches of their sock puppets and puppet theatre.

2. Choose an old, clean sock, preferably knee-high. Avoid socks that are too thin or that have holes. When choosing the sock, let the sock's features be a part of what forms the sock puppet's final character.

3. Glue (using a glue gun and hot melt glue), or sew the googly eyes or buttons, (the number, size and colour of choice), to the bottom of the sock, at the toe end, or wherever children would like!

4. Once the glue is dry, stick a hand inside. Form the hand into the shape of a mouth, with your thumb below the fingers. Use your free hand to force an indentation mirroring the inside of the mouth (arm should look like a snake).

5. For the tongue: use a smaller oval in a different colour to simulate a tongue, or use an actual tongue shape that hangs out. A felt tongue could be made and cut with a 'v' at the end like a snake's tongue.

6. Make a nose using felt. Either sew or glue it into place above the mouth.

7. Add whiskers below the nose by cutting whisker length pieces of string or cord. Sew or stick into place above the mouth. Maybe add a moustache.

8. The same string can be used for hair. Consider a pile of string for hair, or more pieces of felt for spikes, or scales. Glue or sew on ears made out of felt.

9. For arms, simply roll up a length of felt with a pipe cleaner inside. The pipe cleaner will enable you to pose the puppet. Glue the roll closed, with one end attached to the puppet.

10. Finally, add on extra details like eyelashes, hoop earrings, bow ties, hair ribbons and clothes.

What's in it for the children?

Children will have an opportunity to use various skills in individual ways.

Taking it forward

- Ask children to take the sock puppets home and record their stories (what they have done, how they felt etc.) within their homes.

Observation questions

- Can the children link activities and events?

- Do the children show an understanding of a basic storyline?

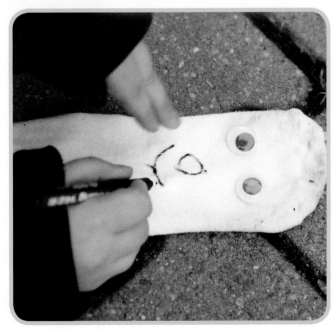

Story box

What you need:

- A shoebox or sweet tin
- Glue
- Plain paper to cover the box
- Sticky tape
- Scissors
- **Decorations** (including coloured paper, wool, egg cartons)
- **Objects related to story** (collected by the children)

What to do:

1. Decide on a story together with the children.
2. Wrap the shoebox in paper.
3. Using scissors, cut a hole through the paper.
4. Children can decorate their box with coloured paper spots or stickers, wool and images which relate to the chosen story.
5. Organise a journey in the garden/park/within the setting and encourage the children to collect objects that tie in with the story, for example: apple, comb, mirror for *Snow White*.

What's in it for the children?

Using specific words when talking about a theme or a story will help children to develop a wider vocabulary. Children will gain a greater understanding of the connection between objects, words and meaning.

Taking it forward

- Organise pop-up theatre events using the story box.
- Children can create their own stories and make a story box to match.

Observation questions

- Does the child ask questions? Can the child pronounce new words?
- Can the child connect words, objects and images?

Story dice

What you need:

- **Square tissue box or other soft cardboard box**
- **Glue**
- **Plain paper to cover the box**
- **White cardboard or paper**
- **Scissors**
- **Decorations** (including coloured paper spots, wool, egg cartons)

What to do:

1. If using a square tissue box, cover all the sides with glue and plain paper.

2. If making the dice from another box cut the box up to create a large flat piece. Draw a cube using a tempate such as this:

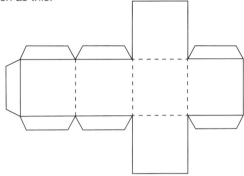

Cut out the cube. Fold the paper, following the dotted lines, and fold the paper inward, making sure to fold the tabs inward as well. Glue the tabs in place.

3. Draw or stick pictures connected to a story the children would like to represent on all sides of the dice.

What's in it for the children?

Stories and rhymes will help children's memory and identification skills. Connecting pictures to stories will help children understand print and how it relates to writing and reading.

Taking it forward

- Children can create their own dice to take home, based on their own favourite story.
- Children can make up a story and images for the die.

Observation questions

- Does the child know any classic stories?
- Can the child connect picture to story?

Story boards

What you need:

- Large card
- Pens
- Pencils
- Crayons
- Ruler

What to do:

1. Make a list of the main events of the story in the order they will be told. Identify the key scenes in the story. You don't need to recreate the entire experience, but demonstrate important key parts that will draw the listener in.

2. Turning points in the story are important to show.

3. Decide how detailed to get. A storyboard can be incredibly detailed when made with older children.

4. The point of the storyboard is to provide visual clarity – a good storyboard will be easily understood by anyone viewing it.

5. Write/discuss a description of what each cell will show, how to depict the action in each illustration, what the important elements are. Take the setting into account as well.

6. Decide which medium to use for the template. For example, a basic storyboard drawn by hand is made by dividing a poster board into empty frames of the same size using a pencil and a ruler. The set-up should look similar to that of a comic book, with rows of square or rectangular cells.

7. Start bringing the scenes to life by drawing the sketches onto the template. Simple stick figures are fine.

8. Older children can write their own description of what's happening in the scene, or make note of the dialogue that takes place.

9. Finalise the storyboard. Once the children have identified the key points of the subject and worked out a design for each frame, they can review their work and make final changes.

10. Encourage them to think in three-point perspective so the images look more like movie scenes: draw characters as though they were standing in perspective.

What's in it for the children?

Children will have an opportunity to work together and negotiate. This will develop their communication skills and vocabulary.

Taking it forward

- Collect old magazines and cut out pictures to use as characters.

- Add children's photos to make it more personal.

- Laminate characters and make the storyboard moveable/changeable.

Observation questions

- Can the children understand the sequence of events?

- Can the children share ideas and listen to those of others?

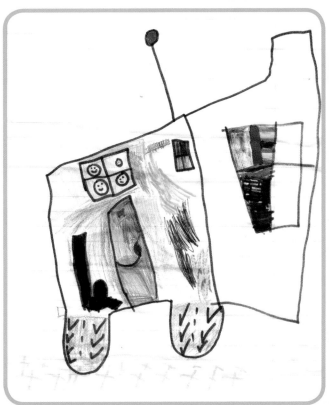

Story dress-up

What you need:

- A large cardboard box
- Fabric, scarves, old pieces of clothing
- Paper in various sizes, colours, construction paper
- Scissors
- Masking tape
- Glue
- Art supplies to decorate: paint, glitter, sequins etc.

What to do:

1. Cut the top off a large cardboard box and decorate it with pictures of classic children's stories.

2. Collect fabric, scarves, old pieces of clothing, old hats, old shoes, gloves etc. to encourage the children to dress up.

3. To make the storyteller's headband: cut a strip of brown construction paper. The strip should be long enough to wrap around the wearer's head with a little extra overlap (roughly 2.5 cm extra to the length) to ensure the ends can be glued together securely once the band has been decorated. Make sure that the paper is fairly thick and heavy.

4. Decorate the band using markers, crayons, or coloured pencils to create a colourful design, inspired by the chosen story. Children can also use oil pastels, acrylic craft paint or poster paint.

5. Encourage the children to act out and discuss the stories in their dress-up garb.

What's in it for the children?

Children will learn to describe the main story setting, developing an understanding of different characters, times and events.

Taking it forward

- Make separate boxes for particular stories, e.g. Little Red Riding Hood box.
- Make boxes suiting different cultures, using stories originating from different countries.
- Add CDs and/or musical instruments.

Observation questions

- Does the child show interest in dressing up?
- Can the child impersonate different characters?
- Does the child use different sounds/tones to differentiate between characters?

Story mats and stones

What you need:

- **A large piece of canvas material in the colour of the background needed** (blue for ocean, green for meadow, brown for woodland etc.)

- **Fabric paint or fabric markers**

- **Stones of all shapes and sizes**

- **Bits of fabric and paper**

- **Hole punch**

- **Scissors**

- **PVA glue**

What to do:

1. Lay out a large piece of canvas fabric (ideally big enough for at least six children to fit around) and paint or draw the background scene, such as trees for the woodland scene, plants, rocks, coral, grass and sand for the water world.

2. Alternatively, sew on pieces of fabric to represent objects.

3. To prepare the story stones: collect smooth stones in a bucket, fill it with water, scrub each one with a brush, then set them out to dry.

4. Next, using a fabric pencil, draw the shape of the chosen character on fabric and cut it out. Find a stone that seems to work well with the character, and coat the stone with PVA glue. Put the fabric character on the stone and paint another layer of glue over it. Use fingers to rearrange the shape, so that it is positioned just right on the stone.

5. Use a hole punch to punch out eyes and glue them on the character. Also add small details such as hair, beard, tail etc. Let the stones dry.

6. Make the character some friends, food, and play things in a similar way.

What's in it for the children?

Children will learn to use their skills to imagine and represent feelings, events and thoughts of others, the character developing the ability to plan, summarise and empathise.

Taking it forward

- Make letter stones to represent characters.

- Make paper collage story mats.

Observation questions

- Does the child manipulate small tools well (such as scissors, a paintbrush)?

- Does the child express ideas and thoughts when creating the characters?

Story food

What you need:

- Small containers
- Food items that are related to stories

What to do:

1. Choose a story and discuss the storyline, the important scenes, the characters and ask the children to think about the food that could be linked to the story, for example:

   - *Goldilocks and the Three Bears* – porridge
   - *Winnie the Pooh* – honey
   - *Snow White* – apples
   - *Baba Yaga* – rice
   - *Alice in Wonderland* – shrinking and growing food
   - *Little Red Riding Hood* – bread

   And many many more (*Princess and the Pea* is an easy one!)

2. Ask the children to collect food items that link to a story.

3. Lay the collected objects in the middle of a table and ask the children to discuss how the food items link to the characters/events of a story.

4. Tell the story together and illustrate it with food.

What's in it for the children?

Children will remember their learning differently from the usual process, as they will be helped by the additional memories, experiences and feelings.

Taking it forward

- Organise a story-related picnic.
- Carry out a story-related taste testing.

Observation questions

- Can the children use their imaginations when handling objects?

Story puzzle

What you need:

- Cardboard boxes in various sizes
- Old poster
- Scissors
- Glue
- Black marker
- Sharp blade/scalpel

What to do:

1. Chose a story.
2. Flatten the cardboard box and cut out a large rectangle.
3. When working with younger children: create (drawing, painting or using decoupage) pictures related to the story on the rectangular base board or glue on a story poster.
4. Mark the puzzle pieces on the rectangle.
5. Create a grid, flip the puzzle over and place it image-side down. Use a ruler to mark out and draw a grid pattern made up of squares that are 5 cm (for a puzzle with fewer, larger pieces).
6. To create the puzzle pieces: draw piece templates on to the grid - begin adding ball and socket shapes (concave and convex half-circles) along the edges of the grid squares so that the pieces will fit into each other when the puzzle is cut. You could also use inverted and protruding triangles, squares, or other shapes.
7. Cut the pieces out with a sharp blade or scalpel (adults only).

What's in it for the children?

The activity will develop children's ability to pay attention to detail and pattern.

Taking it forward

- Make individual puzzles (to take home).
- Use group photos and create your own story on a puzzle.

Observation questions

- Does the child pay attention to detail? Does the child show interest in patterns?
- How long does the child concentrate?

Story rocks and pebbles

What you need:

- Grass
- Pebbles
- Sticks
- Glue
- Tape
- String
- White cardboard or paper
- Scissors
- **Decorations** (including coloured paper spots, wool)

What to do:

1. Select larger pebbles with face or body shape potential. Although really, with some imagination, any pebble can become a face or a body.

2. Looking at characters from a story book, examine specifics of the characters and create facial expressions on the surface of the pebbles with black markers.

3. Collect grass and sticks for hair, ears, eyes, noses and mouths or create them with paper, string and glue.

4. Alternatively, decorate pebbles with paint.

5. Use them to help the children in telling classic or made-up stories.

What's in it for the children?

Children will learn to understand simple instructions when making the pebble people.

Taking it forward

- Children can create their own pebble family, trying to copy the characteristics of their family members

Observation questions

- Can the child follow simple instructions?

Story scarves

What you need:

- A large piece of fleece fabric
- Fabric markers
- Scissors

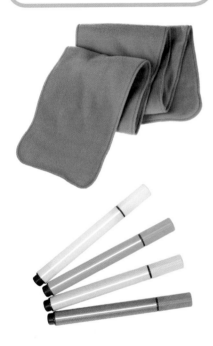

What to do:

1. To make the scarf take a piece of fleece fabric, at least 25 cm long. Lay the fabric on a large table. Fold your fabric in half along its length. Match up the edges as closely as possible. Measure the width of an existing scarf. Scarf length preference varies from person to person: 20 to 25 cm is a standard width for a scarf, 150 cm is the standard length, but 100 cm long would work better for a child.

2. Measure the same width from both edges/ends of the fleece piece and mark the width measurement along the desired length with a pencil. This will create a straight line to cut and ensure a nicer finish for the scarf. Mark the same measurements on the other side of the fleece. Use a straight edge or yardstick to connect the measurements on the length of fabric.

3. Trim the fabric in line with the measurements, using either a rotary cutter or a sharp pair of fabric scissors (adults only). Cut off the curled edges at the bottom of the scarf, using a straight edge to ensure cutting evenly.

4. Make a fringe at the ends of the scarf. Measure 10 cm from the edge of the scarf and mark it with a pencil. Measure and cut strips up to the pencil line every 1 cm.

5. Draw pictures relating to the chosen story along the whole length of the scarf with a fabric marker and ask the children to tell a story using their scarf.

What's in it for the children?

Children can impersonate the characters of the story by wearing the scarf with the story-reminder on, and their memory will develop.

Taking it forward

- Stick a fabric collage onto the scarf to represent the story.
- Paint the scarf with fabric paint.

Observation questions

- Does the child manipulate small tools well (such as scissors, a paintbrush)?
- Does the child express ideas and thoughts when creating the story characters?

Story tents

What you need:

- A large piece of material or lightweight blankets
- Chairs
- Stick or long pole
- Paper clips
- Safety pins
- Wooden pegs
- Rubber bands
- Cushions, pillows, quilts
- Objects related to a story
- Torch

What to do:

1. To make the tent: Arrange the chairs into a square. Place a lightweight blanket over the top of the square. Clip in place, using paper clips, safety pins, rubber bands etc.

2. Ask helpers to pull back each of the chairs until the tent no longer droops in the middle.

3. Insert a stick or pole in the middle, to raise the blanket upwards. Keep the stick in place by pushing large cushions or pillows around it.

4. Lay comfortable items across the floor. Add quilts, cushions, and other comfy things inside.

5. Add objects related to a chosen story such as food, household items, clothing etc.

6. Use a torch to create extra effects, creating an atmosphere and bringing stories to life.

What's in it for the children?

Children will experience close proximity of others, developing an understanding of their physical limitations and that. They will understand basic social rules and practise how to overcome personal boundaries.

Taking it forward

- Prepare boxes of objects to change the scene of the story.

- Create an outdoors tent in a similar way.

Observation questions

- Does the child show schematic play – such as enveloping, transporting?

- Is the child comfortable with the close proximity of others?

Wooden peg puppets

What you need:

- Wooden dolly pegs
- Pipe cleaners
- Felt tip pens in various colours
- Cotton fabric pieces
- Yarn
- Paper doily
- Card in various colours
- Glue
- Glitter, sequins

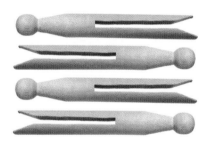

What to do:

1. Decide on the story and characters to make.

2. On the peg, draw the character's eyes, nose, and mouth with felt-tip pens.

3. Wind a pipe-cleaner around the 'neck' of the peg to make two arms. Bend at each elbow.

4. Trim a piece of cotton fabric into a rectangle about 8 cm by 5 cm. Squirt some glue along one edge and wrap it around the figure's body just below the arms to form a tube. Use some more glue to fix it into place at the back.

5. Make a skirt, cut the paper doily from the edge to the centre. Cut a small circle at the centre about the width of the peg. Wrap the doily skirt around the figure and stick it in place with glue.

6. Create hair by cutting out pieces of yarn and sticking them to the figure's head.

7. Draw the shape of extras (like fairy wings, bags, shoes etc.) on card and cut them out. Glue them to the right places.

8. Add glitter and sequins for extra sparkle.

What's in it for the children?

Children will experience the close proximity of others, developing an understanding their physical limitations and that of others. They will understand basic social rules and practise how to overcome personal boundaries.

Taking it forward

- Create a scene for the peg puppets in a cardboard box.
- Make up creative names for the characters.

Observation questions

- Does the child show good hand-eye co-ordination when creating?
- Does the child show well-developed fine muscle control?

Storytelling tree spirit

What you need:

- Pieces of clay
- Leaves
- Sticks
- Natural embellishments

What to do:

1. Choose a story and discuss with the children what characters they will make. Discuss the characteristics of each one, so the children can develop an idea about how to portray their chosen character.

2. Cut or rip a chunk of clay off for each child. The size of clay broken off will determine the size of tree spirit children will make.

3. Roll the clay into a ball and flatten slightly to form a disc.

4. Pat the disc onto the tree trunk. Ask children to place all tree spirits in an arrangement that fits the storyline.

5. Create a face shape and use natural objects to complete the details of the face.

6. Name the spirit and tell the story that goes around the tree.

What's in it for the children?

Children can learn about the world around them using their investigation and observation skills. Noting characteristics and small details such as the patterns on different tree barks, the shapes of different leaves etc. will help children develop observation skills, memory and navigation.

Taking it forward

- Take photos of the spirits and create a very unique story book.

Observation questions

- Does the child talk about some of the things they have observed such as plants, animals, natural and found objects?

- Does the child talk about why things happen and how things work?

Outdoor story trail

What you need:

- **An outdoor area with a variety of surfaces**
- **Rocks in different sizes** (at least ten)
- **Green and brown paint** (for a natural look that does not invade the natural space)

What to do:

1. Find an outdoor area and make a clear map for the children.
2. Choose and discuss the major events of a story (no more than ten).
3. Paint a picture, a scene representing each event on a rock (or you can use cones with paper stuck on if you don't have rocks available). If there are more rocks, add details that refer to where the scene takes place, or a key object (such as woods and basket for Little Red Riding Hood).
4. Place the rocks in a sequence within the chosen area, for the children to walk through and retell the story.
5. Discuss the walk and what they might experience.
6. When on the walk ask children to describe their experiences as well as the story.

What's in it for the children?

When walking or playing outdoors, the richness of the environment offers a wide variety sensory experiences. Through the colours, smells, sounds and visual details of nature children will have opportunity to develop their observation skills, as well as their ability to focus and prioritise.

Taking it forward

- Place objects next to the rocks/cones to make the walk more exciting.
- Encourage the children to dress-up and act out the story.

Observation questions

- Does the child talk about some past and future events (relating to the story or to their own lives)?
- Does the child recognise any special times/events?
- Is the child co-operating? Is the child ready to share information?

Wooden story discs

What you need:

- **Wooden discs** (tree cookies)
- **Glue**
- **Tape**
- **String**
- **White cardboard or paper**
- **Scissors**
- **Decorations** (including coloured paper spots, wool, other art supplies)

What to do:

1. Lay out wooden discs – 'tree cookies' – and decide what characters, scenes, objects the children will portray.
2. Looking at characters, from a story book, examine specifics of the characters, and create facial expressions on the surface of the tree cookies with black markers.
3. Collect grass and sticks for small details or create them with paper, art supplies and glue.
4. Use the tree cookies to help the children in telling classic or made-up stories.
5. They can also be used outdoors.

What's in it for the children?

Children will explore a variety of media from different ages of human history to understand how information can be conveyed in different ways, and how print/text/meaning can connect in different ways.

Taking it forward

- Children can create tree cookies for scenes from their own lives.
- Children can create number and letter tree cookies to use when retelling events.
- Examine how cave drawings told stories.

Observation questions

- Can the child follow simple instructions?
- Does the child explore a variety of media to express thought/ideas?

Story blanket

What you need:

- A thick blanket, or two fleece pieces at least 1.5 m by 1.5 m
- Measuring tape
- Scissors
- Hot melt glue and glue gun
- Decorating materials such as buttons. fabric pieces, fabric pens etc.

What to do:

1. You can buy or make your own blanket for this activity. The optimum size is 2.5 m² for a nice, twin sized blanket.

2. If making your own tie-ended, non-sewn blanket, you will need a piece of fleece 3-4 m in length. Spread out the material completely flat, and then fold it into equal halves. Cut along the fold and trim as necessary to ensure both pieces of fabric are the same size.

3. Keeping the two pieces aligned and together, cut out 5 cm squares from each corner of the material. You may wish to keep the discarded material for use in other activities.

4. Next create small, even fabric ties by making cuts around the edges of each square (still together and evenly aligned) in 2.5 cm intervals.

5. Keeping the two pieces of fabric as flat and smooth as possible, use the ties to join the pieces of material back together.

6. Tighten and re-tie the knots and trim as necessary. You now have a strong two sided blanket for decoration!

7. Use any decorative materials the children wish to make pictures related to their chosen story, (they can direct an adult with the hot glue gun rather than using it themselves). Tell the story together using your fantastic new blanket!

What's in it for the children?

Children can experience the idea of printing, signs and symbols on a large scale. Their understanding of how to convey meaning will grow.

Taking it forward

- Compare the story book and the story blanket and discuss similarities and differences

Observation questions

- Can the children understand the visualisation of events?

- Can the children make connections between a story and pictures?

Story sticks

What you need:

- Thick sticks
- Scissors
- Old colourful magazines
- Glue
- Velcro

What to do:

1. Print pictures or find images in old magazines related to the children's choice of story.

2. Cut out the pictures, laminate them and stick some Velcro on the back.

3. Put a piece of Velcro on the length of the paint stick.

4. As the story is told, ask the children to attach the picture, eg. of character, setting, prop.

5. The stick can also be used as part of a story dialogue. When a child is holding the stick they have uninterrupted time to speak about their view of the story. All children should listen and not interrupt the words or the silence. After some time, the facilitator can ding a little chime and the story stick passes to the next child. After all the children have had a turn, the group can engage in a story dialogue. One person starts and each person adds something as they pass the stick around the circle.

What's in it for the children?

Children can experience the idea of sharing their thoughts and respecting the thoughts of others. They will experience the joy of shared thinking.

Taking it forward

- Use musical instruments to make the storytelling event more colourful and vivid.

- Use the stick together with other aids such as the story blanket and the story scarf.

Observation questions

- Can the children observe silence?

- Can the children respect their friends by listening?

- Are the children ready to share their thoughts?

Story wall art

What you need:

- An empty wall space
- Masking tape or sticky tack
- Large sheets of plain paper or a roll of paper
- Crayons
- Chalk
- Pencils

What to do:

1. Choose a story and discuss the storyline and most important scenes.
2. Secure the paper on a large, empty wall space and encourage the children to make drawings of the story in a chronological sequence.
3. Make a general background setting such as forest, meadow, family house etc. and then draw and cut out figures to create an interactive story wall.

What's in it for the children?

Children can work together on a large scale project and apart from the joy of working together, they will also develop physical strengths, better muscle control and an understanding of their own imitations (how far they can reach etc.).

Taking it forward

- Use puppets and act out the story in front of the wall.

Observation questions

- Can the children remember the story line?
- Can the children translate a story into visual images?

Soundbags for stories

What you need:

- Empty fabric bag such as an old sports bag
- Objects that make various sounds:
  - wooden sticks
  - metal spoon
  - wooden spoon
  - various lids made of metal and plastic
  - plastic bottles and small containers
  - pebbles
  - buttons
  - matchsticks etc.

What to do:

1. Choose a story and discuss the storyline, the important scenes, the characters and ask the children to think about the sounds the characters make (such as the howling of wolf in *The Three Little Pigs*) or the sounds of different events (the blowing the Bid Bad Wolf does, the sound of little pigs' houses crushing etc).

2. Ask the children to collect objects (indoors and outdoors) that will produce different sounds.

3. Lay the collected objects in the middle of a circle and ask the children to discuss what sound they could make for which character with the chosen objects.

4. Tell the story together and illustrate it with sounds.

5. You could have different bags for each story, or a general sound bag that could be used whenever a story is told.

What's in it for the children?

Children can experience shared thinking, and thinking outside the box. They will engage in imaginative and pretend play when using objects differently from their everyday functions.

Taking it forward

- Organise a story sound walk.
- Record voices/noises/sounds to use in storytelling.

Observation questions

- Can the children use their imagination when handling objects?
- Can the children link sounds and stories?

Story scents

What you need:

- Empty fabric bags and small containers
- Things with natural scents:
  - dried herbs
  - flowers
  - spices
  - cocoa powder
  - essential oils
  - citrus fruits
  - coffee
  - dried coconut
  - vanilla pod
  - earth
  - honey

What to do:

1. Choose a story and discuss the storyline, the important scenes, the characters and ask the children to think about the scents that could be linked to the story (eg. bread for *Little Red Hen*, porridge for *Goldilocks and the Three Bears* etc.).

2. Ask the children to collect natural objects (indoors and outdoors) that would produce different smells/scents.

3. Lay the collected objects in the middle of a circle and ask the children to discuss how the scents link to the characters of a story.

4. Tell the story together and illustrate it with scents.

What's in it for the children?

Children can engage in sensory play, enhancing their learning differently from how the information is communicated using audio-visual methods.

Taking it forward

- Make special perfumes for story characters.
- Organise a story-related blind smell-test.

Observation questions

- Do the children use a variety of words to describe their experiences?
- Can the children remember details and descriptions?

Story cupcakes

What you need:

- To make 12 cupcakes:
  - 140 g self-raising flour
  - 140 g butter
  - 140 g sugar
  - 2 tsp vanilla extract
  - 2 eggs
  - 1 egg yolk
  - 3 tbsp milk
- Flavourings that match the story such as:
  - 2 tbsp of porridge for *Goldilocks and the Three Bears*
  - 2 tbsp fresh red berries for *Little Red Riding Hood*
  - an apple chopped finely for *Snow White*
  - some apple, orange, plum chopped finely for *The Very Hungry Caterpillar* etc.
- A muffin tray
- Cupcake cases
- For the butter cream:
  - 115 g butter
  - 250 g icing sugar
- White 'ready to roll' icing (fondant)
- Food colouring in various colours
- Paintbrushes

What to do:

1. To make the cupcakes mix all the ingredients well in a bowl, and add the chosen flavourings. Divide the batter between the cases and bake for 20-22 minutes in a 180°C, preheated oven.

2. Make the buttercream by beating the butter and icing sugar until light and fluffy.

3. Once the cupcakes are cooled, spoon buttercream icing onto the cakes and mould shapes resembling the characters from the chosen story.

4. Children can retell the story, based on the cupcake they chose.

5. Encourage children to use their basic knowledge and their imagination by asking leading questions.

What's in it for the children?

By linking stories to flavours children will learn about making connections in their lives and in the environment. This will help their reasoning skills and their ability to find explanations when facing various situations.

Taking it forward

- Organise story related taste testing, e.g. try different foods that *The Very Hungry Caterpillar* tried, try porridge in different foods linked to *Goldilocks*, try different variations of apple whilst discussing the story of Snow White.

Observation questions

- Does the child show an understanding of how flavours/food can link to stories?

- Is the child able to recall stories and past experience?

Story journey

What you need:

- Paper
- Pencils
- Camera

What to do:

1. Choose a story and discuss the storyline, the important scenes and the characters. Ask the children to think about where the story could take place in their immediate environment.

2. Take the children on a walk in their chosen place and retell the story with them whilst walking.

3. Ask the children to gather objects that they can link to the story (such as shells for *The Little Mermaid*'s beach, a feather for *The Ugly Duckling*'s pond, sticks for the *Three Little Pigs*' house etc.)

4. Retell the story after the walk and share personal experiences and memories.

What's in it for the children?

Children will create their own memories and feelings linked to stories by 'living' the experience of a storyline.

Taking it forward

- Make a story book using the children's photos.

- Dress up and act out the story on the journey.

Observation questions

- Can the children use their imaginations when seeing familiar places in a new light?

- Can the children link places, memories, stories and knowledge?

50 fantastic ideas for storytelling

What you need:

- Tea set
- Blanket
- Real or toy food items such as biscuits, fruit
- Pieces of fabric in various colours

What to do:

1. Choose a story and discuss the storyline, the important scenes and the characters. Ask the children to think about their favourite scene that could be related to food or eating (*Alice in Wonderland* works particularly well).

2. Make special invitations with the children.

3. Ask the children to gather objects that they can link to the story within the tea party.

4. Retell the story during the party and encourage all the children to express their views and share their experience.

What's in it for the children?

Children will have the opportunity to become part of a social circle. Having the storyline as a common talking point might encourage quieter children to be more talkative.

Taking it forward

Invite guests from another educational setting.

Invite the children's family, parents, siblings and grandparents.

Observation questions

- Can the children communicate via stories?
- Can the children link story events to those in their own lives?

Forest school storytelling

What you need:

- Pieces of fabric
- Old bird cages
- Old dresses, pieces of clothing, cloaks
- Old pieces of furniture
- Old pillows and blankets

What to do:

1. Choose a woody area nearby where it's possible to position objects.

2. Take unusual, unexpected indoor items into the natural, forest school environment. The presence of unusual things will invite the children to use their imagination: a dressing up bag, full of unexpected and quirky objects, an old bed, sewing machine, dresses on hangers on tree branches.

3. Add surprises and hidden treasures such as a box of old books, watches, buttons, old glass bottles.

4. Transform your outdoor area: a clearing can be a dining room, and the overhanging trunk of a tree can become a horse by hanging long ropes over it and adding a cardboard box head on the end.

5. Hang small props on huge places to create a tiny fairy garden, such as bird cages, clocks and so on.

6. Make the forest school area a print-rich environment. Include quotes and snippets from stories. Provide blackboards, chalks, clipboards and pencils so the children can make their own marks too.

7. Involve the children in making willow and twig wands or hobby horses from sticks. Sweep the forest floor for a ball with a twig besom (broom).

8. Encourage the children to tell their own stories.

Children will have the opportunity to enjoy the benefits of spending time outdoors, while the surprise elements will aid the development of creativity and complex thinking.

Taking it forward

- Make a fairy post office.

- Organise an elf restaurant.

- Set the scene for a gnome nursery/ school.

Observation questions

- Do the children engage with the scenes?

- Do the children behave the same outdoors as indoors? If differently, how?

A story birthday

What you need:

- Art materials such as:
  - paper
  - pencils
  - crayons
- Balloons
- Crêpe paper
- Coloured card
- String

What to do:

1. Choose a story and discuss the storyline, the important scenes and the characters. Ask the children to think about which of the characters they would like to organise a birthday party for.

2. Make special invitations with the children.

3. Ask the children to gather objects that they can link to the story within the birthday party.

4. Create decorations and decorate a nominated place.

5. Retell the story during the birthday party or create a story about the character's birthday and encourage all the children to express their views and share their experiences.

6. Ask one of the children to act as the chosen character.

What's in it for the children?

Children will have the opportunity to understand the feelings of others and develop empathy while impersonating a story character.

Taking it forward

- Throw story themed birthday parties for the children.

- Create stories about the children and the whole class a character and act them out for the children's birthdays as a surprise present.

Observation questions

- Can the children empathise?

- Are the children ready to celebrate the happiness/achievement of others?

Library trip

What you need:

- **Bus tickets** (if needed)
- **Map of the local area**
- **Identity badges or coloured card**
- **String**
- **Scissors**
- **Felt tip pens**

What to do:

1. Discuss with the children where the local library is.

2. Talk about how the library can be accessed (the journey there, getting in etc.) and how books can be borrowed.

3. Organise the trip (obtain parents' permission, call the library and book an appointment, buy tickets if needed) and chose children for the following roles: map-reader, first aider, note-taker, photographer, caterer (to carry snacks and drinks).

4. Visit the library and chose a story book to read/borrow etc.

5. After the trip recall the events. Share experiences and collate all documents in a scrapbook to create the story of 'Our class visit to the library'.

6. Use the scrapbook to retell the story of the trip.

What's in it for the children?

Linking real events with stories will enable children to understand the historical importance of writing, reading and telling stories.

Taking it forward

- Make a video/movie by capturing moments of the trip.

Observation questions

- Do the children display interest or excitement?

- Do the children notice small details in their environment ? Can the children recall past experiences?

Waterside stories

What you need:

A couple of each:

- Sticks
- Pebbles
- Shells
- Small buckets of sand
- Small buckets of water
- Pieces of string
- Small pieces of fabric
- Feathers

What to do:

1. Set up two stations with a collection of objects related to the seaside/riverbank/sea/river. Make sure the two stations have the same collection of things.

2. Divide your class into two groups and ask the each group to occupy one of the stations.

3. Start children off with a good sentence, such as: 'This story begins on a stormy, grey afternoon on the edge of a cliff overlooking a restless sea/on the edge of a riverbank overlooking a wavy river ...'.

4. Encourage the children to continue the story, using the objects as they would like to make a complete adventure.

5. Share the stories during circle time.

What's in it for the children?

Children will develop communication, listening and negotiating skills. They will engage in shared thinking and group learning.

Taking it forward

- Act out and video the children's stories.
- For younger children provide a known water/sea-themed pictorial story book and add toy characters.

Observation questions

- Do the children express their own ideas?
- What role does the children play (leader, follower, talker, listener, helper etc.)?

The secret life of...

What you need:

- **The children's own comforters** (soft toys or blankets)
- **Story props**

What to do:

1. Stand or sit all the children in a circle.
2. Ask them to place their toy or object and ask a question about it, such as: Where does this Teddy live? What does this comforter think about the washing machine? What does this toy car do when you are asleep?
3. Encourage the child to answer the question.
4. Encourage the other children to ask questions.
5. Help the children with open-ended questions.
6. Record the story, so it can be used or changed from time to time.

What's in it for the children?

The activity will introduce a new vocabulary to children, whilst also encouraging the exploration of feelings and emotions.

Taking it forward

- Take photos of the children's comforters and create a personalised story book.

Observation questions

- Does the child find it easier to tell stories when a personal motivation/link is involved?
- Does the child use a variety of methods to communicate feelings?

Storytelling chair

What you need:

- Inexpensive folding director's chair
- Old large umbrella
- Fabric paint
- Glue
- Glitter
- Bell
- String
- Torch
- Action clapper
- Old large hat

What to do:

1. Borrow/purchase an inexpensive folding 'director's chair'.

2. Inscribe the canvas back with large colourful letters to show its new identity as the setting's storytelling chair.

3. Add a shade parasol by attaching an old umbrella to the side.

4. Imaginative props like a story teller's hat, or make-believe lights and action clapper can help with the storyteller role play.

5. Encourage the children to take turns at being the storyteller and recount their own stories to others.

What's in it for the children?

Children will develop a wider vocabulary whilst their self-confidence will grow.

Taking it forward

- Invite outside storytellers such as the local post person, police officer or nurse to retell stories from their own lives.

- Organise storytelling days where everyone (children and adults) tell stories using objects from home.

Observation questions

- Do the children readily take the storyteller position?

- Are the children good listeners?

Light and dark show

What you need:

- Torches
- Blankets
- Fairy lights
- Candles

What to do:

1. Chose a story that includes day and night or light and dark to tell to the children and discuss the important scenes.

2. Darken the room as much as possible using curtains/blankets/sheets or paper at the windows and door.

3. Set different scenes within the classroom by using different types of lighting to brighten the area.

4. Ask the children to associate important scenes of the story with different areas from the room and encourage them to give reasons for their decisions.

5. Retell and act out the story.

What's in it for the children?

Children will use their senses to gather information leading to richer experiences.

Taking it forward

- Organise a light and dark show outdoors in the twilight or dusk.

Observation questions

- How do the children react to dramatic changes in the environment such as becoming dark?

- Can the children provide accounts of life events in the form of stories?

Story cooking

What you need:

- Small containers
- Food items that are related to stories
- The bread in The Little Red Hen: *(I suggest cup measurements, easier for children)*
  - 2 cups warm water
  - 2 teaspoons yeast
  - 2 teaspoons salt
  - 5-7 cups flour
- Honey muffin for Winnie the Pooh: *(I suggest cup measurements, easier for children)*
  - 2 cups all-purpose flour
  - ½ cup granulated sugar
  - 1 tablespoon baking powder
  - ½ teaspoon salt
  - 1 cup milk
  - ¼ cup unsalted butter, melted
  - ¼ cup honey
  - 1 egg

What to do:

1. Choose an appropriate story such as The Little Red Hen and discuss the storyline, the important scenes and the characters. Ask the children to think about the food that could be linked to the story.

2. To make the bread in The Little Red Hen:
   - Mix the yeast into the water.
   - Combine the salt with three cups of flour.
   - Add the flour/salt to the water, stirring. Add more flour and continue to stir until the dough holds together and is not wet.
   - Put the dough on a clean, floured surface and knead. Keep adding more flour as needed. Knead until smooth.
   - Shape the bread into two or three large loaves or several mini-loaves.
   - Put the seam side down, tuck under the ends and place the loaves on a lightly greased tray.
   - Grease the top, and cover with cling film. Set in a warm place to rise.
   - Let rise until about doubled in size (30-60 minutes, depending on the temperature of the room).
   - Preheat the oven to 200 degrees C.
   - Slash the top of the loaves several times diagonally for that authentic look.
   - Put the loaves in the oven.
   - Set the timer for roughly 15 to 20 minutes or more, depending on the size of the loaves and whether or not they are in tins.

3. To make honey muffins for Winnie the Pooh:

- Preheat oven to 180 degrees C.
- Line a 12-cup muffin tin with paper cases or spray with a non-stick cooking spray.
- In a large bowl, whisk together the flour, sugar, baking powder and salt.
- In a medium bowl, whisk together the milk, butter, honey and egg.
- Pour the wet ingredients into the dry ingredients and, using a rubber spatula, fold together until no dry ingredients remain.
- Divide the batter evenly between the muffin cases.
- Bake for 12 to 15 minutes, or until a toothpick inserted in the centre comes out clean.
- Cool in the tray for 5 minutes, then remove to a wire rack. Serve warm or at room temperature.

4. Ask the children to discuss how the food items link to the characters/events of the story.

5. Re-telll the story together anduse the food as props.

What's in it for the children?

Children will remember their learning better when linked with memories, experiences and feelings. They will enjoy sharing with their friends, whilst also connecting the different types of knowledge (social, personal, literacy, physical).

Taking it forward

- Children can devise their own story and story-related recipes.
- Organise a food sharing party with items brought from home where children can also share the story of preparing their goods.

Observation questions

- Can the children link food and stories?
- Can the children use their imaginations?

Make your own story video

What you need:

- Large card
- Images from old magazines
- Pens, pencils
- Old fabric, sheets, clothing
- Story props
- Camera or camera phone

What to do:

1. Choose or make up a story and discuss the storyline, the important scenes and the characters.

2. Make a large poster of the storyline. Think of the characters, cut pictures from old magazines and create a plot (plan which scenes you would like capture on video).

3. Share out the roles and decide who will play who in the story video. Decide whether the characters will talk or not, what they will say etc.

4. Create the costumes from pieces of fabric and old clothing.

5. Gather story props (such as a shoe for *Cinderella*, a rose for *Beauty and the Beast* etc.).

6. Rehearse the story.

7. Video the story, pausing at each scene to help the children act.

8. Download and share the story video.

What's in it for the children?

Children will need to recall lots of previous information to organise their video recording such as remembering the storyline, acting, videoing. This will develop their communication, co-operation skills and planning.

Taking it forward

- Children can make a video at home and present it in school.

Observation questions

- Do the children show an ability to co-operate?

- Can the children take different roles in group work?

Storytelling stickers

What you need:

- **Sticky tape and paper or sticky back sheets**
- Pens
- Pencils
- Camera

What to do:

1. Choose or make up a story and discuss the storyline, the important scenes and the characters.

2. Create attachable images of the characters in the story.

3. Attach pictures to each child (randomly or based on the children's choice) and ask them to act accordingly for about 30 minutes.

4. Take pictures or video them and share/discuss their actions during circle time.

5. Encourage the children to extend their play and explore new characters by swapping out their stickers.

What's in it for the children?

Through this activity the children will understand the power of representation in stories, and through using a variety of media such as paper, images, and words, acting children will gain experiences in how to use personal storytelling to study and process life events and feelings. The experience of "being in someone else's place" will develop their social skills such as sympathy and empathy.

Taking it forward

- Children can make their own stickers.
- Use ready-made stickers and make up relevant stories.

Observation questions

- Do the children follow instructions?
- Can the children place themselves in different roles for extended periods of time?

Mime story show

What you need:

- Dressing up clothes or large pieces of fabric
- Scarves, gloves
- Additional items and story props

What to do:

1. Choose or make up a story and discuss the storyline, the important scenes and the characters.

2. Ask the children to act out the story but without making a noise or talking. Help them to pick out relevant dressing up items/props to help tell the story..

3. Watch story videos, movies, documentary films without the sound and try to guess what is happening.

4. Discuss the experience.

What's in it for the children?

Children will begin to understand the importance of non-verbal communication. They will develop empathy towards people who live with hearing disabilities.

Taking it forward

- Children can act out different events without talking or making noises.

- Make a silent story to show outdoors.

- Observe how animals communicate.

Observation questions

- Do the children use non-verbal ways to communicate?

- Do the children show empathy towards the way others communicate?

Story sportsday

What you need:

- Children's books with sports related stories
- Sport equipment such as:
  - hoola hoops
  - balls
  - skipping ropes
  - large baskets, etc

What to do:

1. Choose stories with types of sport or movement in their storyline such as *The Tortoise and the Hare* or *The Gingerbread Man*.

2. Organise the outdoor area to match the story.

3. Create various stations (corners/sections) where the activities take place such as:
   - Hopscotch
   - Shooting aim with ball
   - Skiing simulation with sticks
   - Jumping in a pretend puddle (made from brown card) etc.

4. Alternatively, chose many stories and discuss with the children how they imagine the characters would move (such as Gingerbread man running, Jack climbing, Gruffalo stomping feet, etc.) and organise stations accordingly.

5. Encourage the children to dress up to add to the atmosphere of the event.

What's in it for the children?

Children will have the opportunity to connect their skills (listening, storytelling, remembering, physical movement etc.) and show complex understanding of their own lives.

Taking it forward

- Organise sponsored sports competitions and support charities.
- Organise a 'funny movements' sports day and create a story book using photos of the event.

Observation questions

- Does the child show well developed physical skills?
- Does the child follow simple instructions?
- Does the child participate in physical games?

Shadow storytelling

What you need:

- Computer or books to source silhouettes for the puppets
- Printer to print out figures found on the computer, or tracing paper to trace from books
- Black cardstock to make final puppets
- Scissors, craft knife and cutting mat (a pile of newspaper makes a great cutting mat)
- Wooden or bamboo skewers
- Electrical tape (black) or masking tape
- Halogen/LED lamp, or any source of light that can easily be directed as desired
- White cloth (such as a flat bed sheet) or roll of drawing paper to use as a screen
- Pins, adhesive paper tape or spring tension rod to hang the screen on
- Large piece of cardboard
- Optional: musical instruments or objects to make noises

What to do:

1. Choose or make up a story and discuss the storyline, the important scenes and the characters.

2. Create shadow puppets: find pictures to represent the characters, print/cut them out and trace them on black card. Cut out the card silhouettes and attach them onto the wooden skewers with tape.

3. Use a doorframe to make the screen by pinning a large sheet of paper (from a drawing paper roll) on the frame or hang a piece of cloth (such as a sheet) from a spring tension rod. It's important to make the screen flat.

4. Alternatively, use a portable coat rack. Hang a white bed sheet tightly around the coat rack and fix it to the frame with hair clips or clothes pegs.

5. Place the light source at the back of the white screen.

6. Also create a 'dark' place for the puppet masters to work. Prop a large piece of cardboard or bulletin board against the bottom part of the screen to block the shadows in that area and create a 'stage'. This will hide the children as they sit on the floor behind the screen and move the puppets.

What's in it for the children?

Children will enjoy the fun of being in charge of events. The mystery of the shadows will create a magical experience, whilst having to retell a story will develop the children's, communication, speech and learning skills.

Taking it forward

- Children can video their puppet show to make a story movie.

- Children from the audience can take photos of the scenes and create a story book later.

Observation questions

- Do the children enjoy new situations?

- Can the children both express themselves and listen to others?

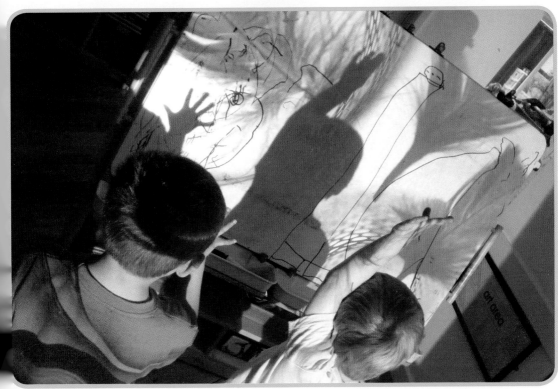

Story treasure hunt

What you need:

- An outdoor area
- A map of the area
- Paper
- Pens, pencils
- Small containers

What to do:

1. Find an outdoor area and make a clear map for the children, using lines but not landmarks, so they will be able to mark important places on as they go.

2. Choose a story and discuss what the major events of the story are.

3. Take the children on a walk following the map and encourage them to gather objects related to the story.

4. Discuss the walk, and what they might have experienced.

5. When on the walk ask children to describe their experiences as well as the story.

What's in it for the children?

Children will have the opportunity to learn new skills. By having to focus on different things simultaneously (such as the storyline, the walk, instructions from adults, the environment etc.), children's ability to concentrate and prioritise will develop.

Taking it forward

- Place unexpected objects on the chosen journey in advance.
- Challenge the children by asking them to find hidden treasures.

Observation questions

- Does the child show observational skills?
- Does the child pay attention to detail?

Water and sand tray story

What you need:

- Builder's tray or very large shallow container
- Soil
- Sand
- Pebbles
- Moss, leaves, sticks, fern and other small plants
- Rocks
- Corks
- Wooden discs (tree cookies)
- Other natural additions such as pine cones, conkers
- Small world characters

What to do:

1. Discuss the children's favourite stories.
2. Place the builder's tray/container safely on a table or on the ground.
3. Scatter sand around in half of the tray, pour water into the other half (you can separate the two halves with pebbles) then organise the plantation.
4. Place small world play characters around the tray and encourage the children to act out their favourite story.
5. Allow plenty of space for the children.
6. Encourage children to think imaginatively and to find items to represent other objects, for example, a twig from the outdoor area to use as a tree.

What's in it for the children?

Children will be able to tell their own stories talking about key characters and sequencing events, work alone or co-operatively, talk about their ideas and negotiate roles with others, whilst engaging in imaginative play.

Taking it forward

- Make clay figurines to use in the play scene.
- Take photos of the children's play and make a story book.

Observation questions

- Does the child happily manipulate the materials?
- Does the child lead, listen or follow the activity?

Story circle

What to do:

1. Stand or sit all the children in a circle with one child named as the starter.

2. Give the starter child a toy or object and say a sentence about that subject, such as:

   - This little horse went to nursery one day...

   - The pine cones come to the park across the street, where one day we...

   - In my house there are wooden spoons like that, and usually for dinner...

3. Encourage the starter child to finish the sentence.

4. Encourage the next child in the circle to carry on.

5. Help the children with open-ended questions.

6. Record the story, so it can be used or changed from time to time.

What's in it for the children?

This activity to encourages children to develop their vocabulary and use of language, but also helps them understand their feelings and emotions.

Taking it forward

- Ask the children to retell familiar stories in a circle.

Observation questions

- Does the child use an extended vocabulary?

- Does the child pay attention to events and follow the sequence?

Family stories

What you need:

- Old family photos from the children's family
- Historical memoirs
- Photos from the lives of famous historical characters

What to do:

1. Consider some of the children's family stories. Ask parents to talk to their relatives and conduct some basic genealogical research.

2. Find an interesting character or story in their past and create stories about them or tell their true stories.

3. Research family stories that have been passed down, such as: Did their grandma have any sayings? Do family members have special jokes about past event? What food does their uncle like? and so on.

4. Invent a character for storytelling and use incidents and insights from the children's own past to create adventures for the character.

5. Encourage children to tell the story in the first person point of view (using 'I'). Think about the lessons they have learned or funny, interesting things that have happened to them over the years. Turn these events into compelling stories.

What's in it for the children?

Apart from sparking the imagination of children, this activity will develop their ability to bond and build relationships.

Taking it forward

- Invite the children's family members into your setting to tell stories.

Observation questions

- Does the child understand the connection between past and present?

- Is the child showing interest in their own family history?

Stories in rhymes and songs

What you need:

- Story props such as puppets, toys

What to do:

1. Discuss with the children what songs and nursery rhymes they know.

2. Identify the characters in the stories and discuss what happens to them.

3. Tell their story as a tale, rather than a song.

4. Add the usual story elements, such as: starting with 'Once upon a time', find a main character, add a start/crisis, solution/end frame to the story. Add surprising parts, such as a mysterious characters or strange endings.

5. Here is a story about Humpty Dumpty:

Once upon a time there was a good, well-known family, the Dumptys. They had six children, who all loved going to school, but their youngest, Humpty was cheeky and mischievous. He often got into all sorts of trouble. He climbed up trees, walked along fences, soared into the air from rooftops, ran down slopes ... causing his mother, Mrs Dumpty many scared moments. She always said: 'Humpty, Humpty, you will hurt yourself one day...'. 'Oh no mother, I am well rounded, like an egg, so I can roll off anywhere.'

On a sunny August afternoon Humpty and his best egg friend, Eggy decided not top finish their homework and instead went to climb the local church which seemed much more fun. So they walked up to the wall encompassing the church garden, and begin to climb. Humpty sat on the top of the wall, teasing Eggy... 'Catch me if you can...' As he looked down, all of a sudden, he had a great fall, and broke to pieces.

Eggy was really horrified, and ran to the Dumpty's house: 'Mr Dumpty! Humpty had a great fall from a wall!' he shouted. Mr Dumpty run to the castle, to fetch the king's horses and men, who were famous for their healing power. The horses took the men to the place of the accident, but they were unable to put Humpty together again. Mr and Mrs Dumpty, from then on, taught their children not to climb on the wall of the church garden. But what happened to Eggy?

6. Discuss the story of the nursery rhyme and where it originates from (for older children).

Humpty Dumpty was first printed in 1810. At the time, a humpty dumpty was a clumsy person, so the nursery rhyme was meant as a riddle. It doesn't actually state that Humpty Dumpty is an egg, so the aim of the reader is to guess what he really is. Of course there are not many people these days who know he is not an egg. There is speculation that the nursery rhyme had an underlying meaning – in which Humpty Dumpty represents King Richard III of England and the wall his horse. Others have suggested that it refers to the downfall of Cardinal Wolsey at the hand of King Henry VIII.

What's in it for the children?

Children will have the opportunity to think about things in a different context, to think outside the box. They will gather interesting pieces of information and gain historical knowledge, to develop their understanding of modern life as well.

Taking it forward

- Act out the nursery rhyme and dress up as the characters.

Observation questions

- Are the children able to convert a song/rhyme into text?

- Do the children use their imagination to complete the story?

Local tales

What you need:

- Old family photos from the children's family
- Historical memoirs
- Photos from the lives of famous historical characters

What to do:

1. Arrange a visit to a local home for elderly people and encourage the children to talk to the residents.

2. Consider the elderly people's family stories by helping the children ask questions such as: When you were a child..., What did your mummy read to you when ... Where did your daddy work before you... and so on.

3. Record their stories.

4. Discuss the elderly people's past, and together with the children invent a character for storytelling, using incidents and insights the elderly person told them to create adventures for the characters.

5. Encourage children to tell the story in their own words.

What's in it for the children?

Listening to other people's stories will extend the children's knowledge about the world and so their understanding of different cultures and traditions will grow.

Taking it forward

- Invite elderly people into the nursery.
- Make story books as presents.

Observation questions

- Does the child show signs of empathy?
- Does the child listen well?

Stories of 1001 days

What you need:

- Photos of the group/class from the previous year, including all seasons, times of the days and major events, organised into chronological order

- Copies of the stories in *Arabian Nights*

What's in it for the children?

Scientists have found that children who have regular and strong connection to fiction find it easier to understand other people – they show more empathy and have better developed theory of mind (the ability to understand that other people have different thoughts and feelings from us, which is essential for understanding and predicting other people's thoughts and behaviour).

Taking it forward

- Act out the group's own story collection and invite an audience to watch.

- Make story books from the collection.

Observation questions

- Does the child understand feelings of self? Can the children talk about feelings? How they use their vocabulary to describe feelings and differentiate between various stages of feelings such as sad, upset and miserable?

- Does the child show an understanding of the feelings of others?

What to do:

1. Introduce the notion of the '1001 Night' stories to the children by reading them some simple versions. Explain how the storyteller, Scheherezade tries to save herself through stories, telling each of the *Arabian Nights* tales in order to survive a little longer at the mercy of her listener, the Sultan. Highlight how stories can preserve time and memories.

2. Look at class photos from the previous years(s) and consider the stories captured by the images.

3. Tell and record the stories, titled accordingly, such as 'The Tales of 110 class days' etc.

4. Children can all become characters in a story that is about the life of the class, such as the story of the Lost Sandwich – about how John lost his sandwich on the day of the class outing...when he got to the park he could not find it, as the school's pet dog cheekily took it from his bag...

5. Encourage the children to tell the story in their own words.

6. Alternatively, choose their favourite stories from the *Arabian Nights* collection and make the group's stories based on their storylines.

Storytelling through art

What you need:

- An easel
- Paper
- Paint

Taking it forward

- Take photos of the pictures to create a story book.
- Organise an exhibition.

Observation questions

- Can the children paint without talking? Are they able to use various methods of communication?
- Do the children understand their own ability to communicate without words?

What to do:

1. Choose a story and discuss the storyline and the important scenes.

2. Secure sheets of paper on the easel and encourage the children to make images of the scenes and of what they found important in the story.

3. Challenge the children by asking them not to talk whilst painting.

4. Alternatively, place the children's previous drawings scattered on the easel, and ask them to tell a story that includes all the images.

What's in it for the children?

Children can discover their deeper thoughts and their inner world through the focus on the artistic creation process, without the usual communication channel – speech.

Musical storytelling

What you need:

- CD player
- Classical music CDs
- Objects that make various sounds:
  - wooden sticks
  - metal spoon
  - wooden spoon
  - various lids made of metal and plastic
  - plastic bottles and small containers
  - pebbles
  - buttons etc.

What to do:

1. Choose a piece of classical music and ask the children to listen to it carefully.

2. Discuss with them what this song/music might be about. To aid the start of storytelling, introduce a character, according to the title of the piece (for example the swan from the lake, the nutcracker etc).

3. Ask the children to tell a story about the character as you replay the music.

4. Record the story and read it to the children later.

What's in it for the children?

The stories children hear shape their view of the world. Most small children live their lives in quite a limited environment. Stories can show them far-flung places, extraordinary people and eye-opening situations to expand and enrich their world.

Taking it forward

- Watch the recording of an opera or ballet.

Observation questions

- Does the music inspire children to recall life events from the past?
- Do the children use their everyday experiences to imagine the world represented by the piece of music?

Story jars

What you need:

- Various small toy and real other objects
- Large empty jars or containers
- Rice or other small grains

What to do:

1. Fill an empty jar/container with rice or other grains and hide small toys inside. Leave enough space, so the children can put their hands in to grab an object.

2. Sit all the children in a circle and ask a child to grab a toy or object from the jar and say a sentence or ask a question about the object, such as: Where did this object go before coming to our nursery? One afternoon this pen wrote to the queen... and so on.

3. Encourage the children to finish the sentence or answer the question, giving all the children a turn.

4. Support the children with open-ended questions.

5. Record the story, so it can be used or changed from time to time.

What's in it for the children?

The activity can be a great way of helping children deal with real-life situations that they need help with. Researchers have found that the brain activity that occurs when fiction is heard is very similar to experiencing that situation in real life, so telling/listening about a situation helps children work out how to solve it in reality.

Taking it forward

- Encourage the children to create their personal story jar containing objects from home

- Create themed story-jars based on classic stories, on a certain colour or on subjects as home, nursery, doctor's surgery etc.

Observation questions

- Does the child describe real life situations in their storytelling?

- Do the children use their imaginations to complete stories?

- Does the child show understanding of the difference between the real and make believe world?